KU-515-304

Contents

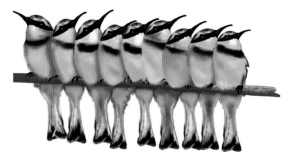

Packaging & Designer: Q2A Design Studio.

© 2003 Grandreams Books Ltd. First published by Grandreams Books Ltd 2003, 4-5 North Parade, Bath

All rights reserved. No part of this publication may be reproduced, stored in a retrieval system or transmitted by any means, electronic, mechanical, photocopying or otherwise, without the prior permission of the publisher.

Printed in China

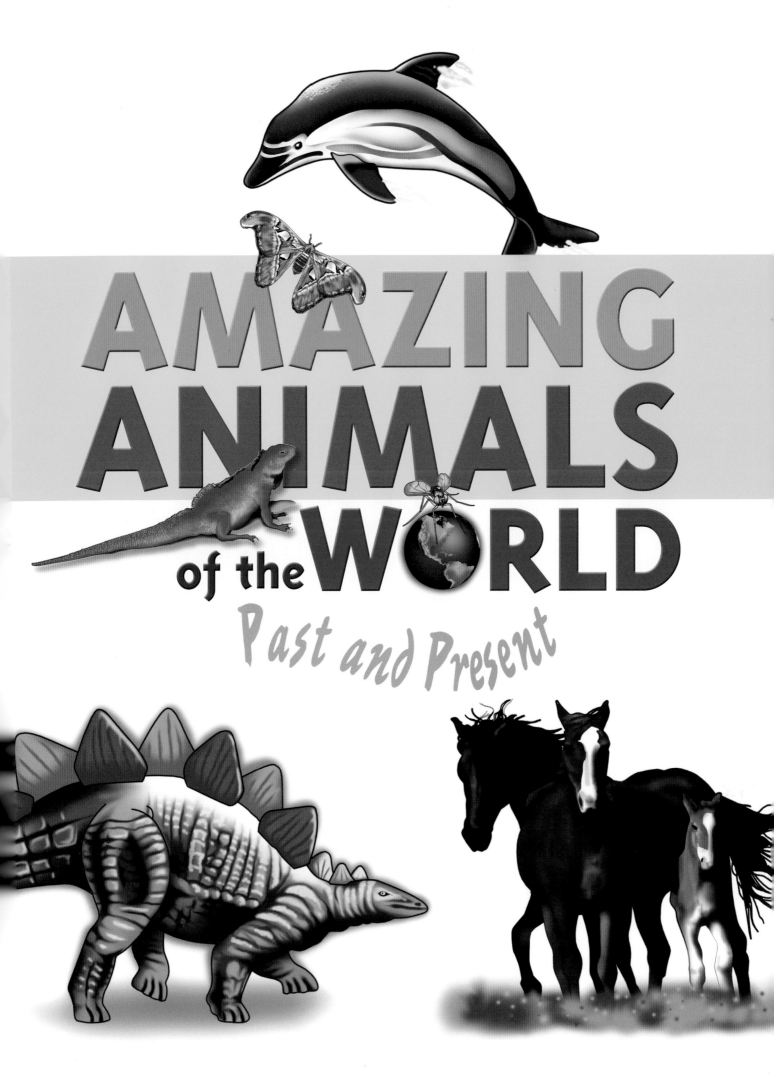

AMAZING ANIMALS
of the WORLD
Past and Present

What kinds of animals are there?

There are two kinds of animals. The ones with backbones are called vertebrates and those without backbones are called invertebrates. Invertebrates form 95 per cent of all animals on the Earth.

What is a mammal?

Mammals are warm-blooded creatures. They all have backbones, and some grow hair or fur on their bodies. They feed their young on milk produced by the mother. Apes, cats, dogs, tigers, elephants, gorillas and horses are all mammals.
So are humans.

What is hibernation?

Many animals that live in the colder regions solve the problem of winter scarcity of food and low temperatures by sleeping in the winter.
To prepare for hibernation, they eat large amounts of food in the summer and build fat that keeps them warm and nourishes them throughout the winter.

What are primates?

Primates are members of the highest order of mammals, which includes man and apes.

What are warm-blooded animals?

Warm-blooded animals can maintain a constant body temperature, irrespective of the outside temperature. Mammals and birds are warm-blooded animals.

Which are the vertebrates?

Vertebrates include all mammals, birds, reptiles, amphibians and fish which have a backbone.

What are monotremes?

The monotremes are primitive egg-laying mammals. The duck-billed platypus and the spiny anteater echidna are the only two monotremes and are found in Australia.

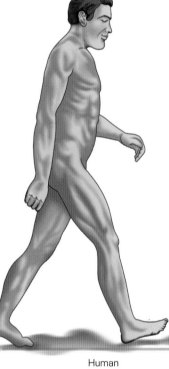

Human

Bird

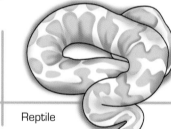

Reptile

Fish

What do animals eat?

There are two main kinds of animal — herbivores and carnivores. Those that eat plants are herbivores.
Deer, horses and pandas are herbivores. Animals that eat meat are called carnivores. Dogs, tigers and lions are carnivores. Animals that eat both plants and meat are omnivores and animals that eat insects are called insectivores.

What are marsupials?

Marsupials are also mammals.They give birth to poorly developed young ones and carry their babies in an abdominal pouch called a marsupium. Kangaroos and koalas are marsupials.

Which are the invertebrates?

Insects, spiders, crabs, worms, jelly-fish and corals are all invertebrates.

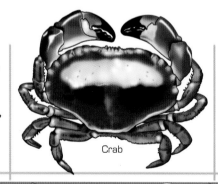

Insect

Spider

Crab

Jelly-fish

Puma

What is a wild cat?

Lions, tigers, cheetahs and leopards belong to the cat family and are usually known as wild cats.

What is the difference between a jaguar and a leopard?

Jaguars are the largest members of the cat family in South America. Even though both jaguars and leopards have yellowish-brown coats with black patterns, the jaguar's spots have irregular shapes. Jaguars are also heavier and have shorter tails. Both black leopards and black jaguars are called panthers.

Which is the most agile member of the cat family?

The pumas are the most agile of them all. They are found mostly in the western parts of America. They can jump, climb trees and surprise their prey with their speed and agility. They are known to cover 18 metres in a single leap.

What is a lion's 'pride'?

Lions are the only members of the cat family that live in large groups called 'prides'. A pride may consist of about two males and seven females and a variable number of cubs. The total could be about 30-40 lions.

Which member of the cat family has the largest teeth?

Clouded leopards have the biggest canine teeth of all the members of the cat family. Their canines can be more than 4cm (1.5 in) long, and they can kill their prey with a single bite.

Siberian Tiger

Who is the 'King of the jungle'?

The lion is called 'the King of the jungle.' It is the only cat with a tufted tail (both sexes) and mane (males). Its roar can be heard up to 9 kilometres away.

Which is the fastest land animal?

Cheetahs are the fastest land animals. These long-legged cats can run up to 110 kilometres per hour (70 mph). However, they can run at this speed for only a few hundred yards.

Which animal is the largest in the cat family?

The male Siberian tiger, which is over 3.048 metres(10 ft) long and weighs up to 300kg (661.3lb), is the largest and the most powerful member of the cat family!

If two tigers met on neutral territory, how would they greet each other?

If there is no quarrel over food or territory, the tigers may greet each other by rubbing their head, chin, cheeks and tails.

How are its stripes useful to a tiger?

The stripes on the tiger's body help it to hide very well in tall grasses when it is waiting to pounce upon its prey.

Lion

3

mighty beasts

What kinds of elephants are there?

There are only two kinds of elephants — those found in Africa and Asia.

How does an African elephant differ from an Asian one?

The African elephant is bigger in size. It also has larger ears and tusks. The African elephant also has a dip between its fore and hind quarters which gives a curvature to its back.

How long do elephants live?

Elephants are known to live for 60 to 70 years.

How do elephants talk to each other?

Elephants talk to each other by making sounds called 'tummy rumbles'. However, these rumbles are so low that humans cannot hear them. They also make a 'trumpeting' sound to call each other.

What is unusual about the hippopotamus?

A hippopotamus spends most of its time in water and can be found in major rivers and swamps. Even babies are born and nursed underwater. Water cools its body and prevents dehydration. The hippo is a good swimmer and the only animal that dares to swim in the same water as crocodiles! It can stay underwater for up to 30 minutes.

Panda

What do pandas eat?

Pandas mainly eat bamboo shoots and leaves. They spend about 12 hours a day eating and can consume 11.7 to 14 kilograms (26 33 lb) of bamboo in a day.

Why is the hippopotamus said to be thick-skinned?

The skin of the hippo is really thick — it can grow up to 5.08 centimetres (2 in) thick in some places. It forms a protective covering for the hippopotamus, and protects it from any attacks from enemies.

What does the elephant do with its trunk?

The elephant uses its trunk to breathe, smell, touch, hold, eat, drink and to caress its young ones. Its trunk is about 2.1 metres (7 ft) long and can suck in 8 litres (14 pints) of water at one time. Elephants cool themselves by spraying water and dust over their bodies. They can even put their trunks into their mouths and extract water from their stomachs and they use it to communicate.

How are elephants useful to us?

Elephants are so important to us that if we lose them, many other animals and plants will also die. They are used as draft animals for hunting and transportation. Ivory from their tusks is used to manufacture jewellery but this is illegal.

What kinds of bears are there?

There are eight kinds of bears — American bears, polar bears, pandas, asiatic bears, sloth bears, spectacled bears, sun bears and grizzly bears.

Where are sun bears found?

They live in the tropical rainforests of South East Asia. They are also called honey bears because of their weakness for honey. Sun bears are the smallest bears in the world but are known to be highly aggressive.

Sunbear

Which animal is considered to be the most intelligent?

Chimpanzees are considered the most intelligent non-human animals. They are also very similar to us in appearance and in their social behaviour.

Baby Chimpanzee

Chimpanzee

Where are gorillas found ?

Gorillas are found in the jungles of Africa and are very large animals. They have long arms, short legs, a wide chest, a big head, large teeth and no tail. They are very gentle animals.

How do chimpanzees use tools?

Like humans, chimpanzees also use tools. They use sticks to bring out ants from their holes and leaves to scoop water. They also use stones to break open nuts.

Squirrel Monkey

Which is the largest animal to live in trees?

The Bornean orangutan, also known as the 'old man of the forest', is the largest animal that lives in trees.

Mandrill

How did the bonnet macaque get its name?

As the name suggests, the bonnet macaque appears to be wearing a hat, due to the strange style of its fur. It has a well-formed cap-like whorl of hair radiating outward from the centre of the head.

Why are spider monkeys so named?

Spider monkeys get their name because of their long, spidery limbs. Their tail acts like a fifth limb with which they can grip the branches of the trees while swinging.

What is so strange about the sounds that squirrel monkeys make?

Squirrel monkeys are among the most vocal of primates. They can chirp, scream, peep, squawk, purr and also bark.

What are the Japanese macaques famous for?

The Japanese macaque is a medium-sized monkey with long, yellowish-grey fur and a bright red face. They are famous for imitating each other's behaviour, much the way humans do.

Which mammal is considered to be the most colourful?

Mandrills, which are found in Africa, are perhaps the most colourful mammals in the world.

Which is the smallest monkey in the world?

The pygmy marmoset is the smallest monkey in the world. It is only 38.10 centimetres (15 in) long including a 17.78 centimetres (7 in) long tail and lives in the forests of South America.

Which animals are considered to be the noisiest?

The noisiest land animal in the world is the howler monkey found in Central and South America. Its screams can be heard 4.83 kilometres (3 miles) away.

it's a dog's life

Which animals belong to the dog family?

Wolves, foxes, jackals, coyotes and dogs belong to the same family. It's called the Canidae family.

Hyena

What are coyotes?

Coyotes resemble a small German shepherd dog and are the wild relatives of the common dog. They are considered to be clever animals because they can adapt to their surroundings, outwit their competitors easily and survive on a wide range of foods.

Coyote

What are hyenas?

The hyena is a doglike carnivore that is a renowned scavenger. Most active at night, hyenas typically scavenge the kills of other animals, feeding on the body parts left behind. They have powerful jaws which can bite through tough hides and crush and digest large bones that other predators cannot eat.

What kind of hunters are hyenas?

Hyenas are considered to be among the most dangerous hunters. Besides feeding on leftovers, hyenas also make their own kills, preferably during the night. Individual hyenas attack small animals, but will form packs of 10 or more to bring down a bigger animal like the zebra.

Which dog does not bark?

The Basenji, a hunting dog which is 43 centimetres (16.93 in) in height and 11 kilograms (24.25lb) in weight, is the only dog which does not bark.

Where would you find a dingo in the wild?

A dingo is the wild dog of Australia. It has a short-haired coat, usually yellowish in colour, but sometimes white, black, brown or rust, a bushy tail, erect ears and a sharp muzzle.

Which are the tallest and smallest dogs?

The great Dane is the tallest dog and can be 81 centimetres (31.89 in) in height, while the chihuahua is the smallest — just 13 centimetres (5.12 in) in height.

Wolves

What is a hoof?

A hoof is a curved covering of horn that corresponds to a nail or claw, but actually in some animals hooves substitute feet. All equids — asses, horses and zebras — are hoofed mammals.

Horses

Antelope

Which is the largest antelope?

The eland is the world's largest antelope. Males have twisted horns that are thick and tightly spiralled.

Which are the wild horses?

Only zebras, wild asses and Przewalski's horses of Mongolia are true wild horses. Wild horses are found today in Africa and Asia.

Where would you bump into antelopes?

Mostly in Africa and sometimes in Asia, where you will come across Nilgai (or bluebuck), Chousingha (four-horned antelope), the blackbuck and a few gazelles. Antelopes vary in size greatly and are generally fairly slender, graceful animals that resemble deer.

Where is the Sika deer found?

The Sika deer is native of Eastern Asia. They all have white spots, which distinguish them from other species of deer. While males carry antlers that average 28-48 centimetres (11.02-18.90 in) in length, females have a pair of black bumps instead. Their fur can range from chestnut-brown to reddish-olive, yellow-brown, tan or grey.

Who are the jumping jacks?

Springboks and many other types of gazelles in Africa leap as high as 3 metres (9.84 ft) from the ground and they leap for all kinds of reasons — if they see an enemy or to warn other springboks of danger or, maybe, just by habit. This special kind of leaping is called 'stotting'.

Why should the domestic donkey pay respects to the African wild ass?

Because the African wild ass is the ancestor of the domestic donkey. It is found in several African countries and can go without water longer than other equids.

Are giraffes noisy?

Giraffes are usually silent, but when they are vocal they make a short roaring sound.

Which is the tallest animal in the world?

Natives of Africa, giraffes are the tallest animals in the world. Giraffes can grow up to 6 metres (19 ft) tall and weigh 1270 kilograms (2,800 lb). A large giraffe can have a neck up to 198 centimetres long (6½ ft). Their height helps them reach tree tops to get their food.

Zebra

What happens if you combine the horse, the zebra and the giraffe?

You come up with what is commonly known as the okapi. Found in the tropical forests of Africa, the okapi has a horse-like upper body and legs with zebra stripes. But it actually belongs to the giraffe family. It is also sometimes called the 'forest giraffe'.

reptiles

What is a reptile?

A reptile is an animal with tough, dry skin covered with horny scales. Turtles, lizards, snakes, crocodiles and alligators are some of the most widespread living reptiles. Reptiles are vertebrates. Like birds, most reptiles hatch from eggs that are laid on land, covered by a protective shell. They breathe air with lungs.

Where can you find reptiles?

Reptiles are found in a broad range of habitats, from the bottom of ponds and lakes to the tree lines of high-elevation alpine regions. However, they are especially abundant and diverse in the tropics and in deserts. Since they cannot generate their own body heat, no reptiles are found in icy Antarctica or the polar regions and very few live within the Arctic Circle.

What is unique about the skin of reptiles?

The skin of reptiles is neither moist nor permeable like that of amphibians, nor feathered like that of birds, nor covered with hair like that of mammals. It is tough and dry, with horny scales.

Which is the longest snake?

The Asiatic reticulated python is the longest snake in the world. It lives in Southeast Asia and is over 8 metres (26 ft) long.

Which is the largest snake?

The anaconda is the heaviest and the most powerful snake in the world. Unlike other snakes which lay eggs, female anacondas give birth to living young.

How are reptiles different from other vertebrates?

Reptiles are cold-blooded. This means that, like amphibians, they are unable to produce their own body heat, so they rely on the sun for warmth.

Why does a rattlesnake rattle?

The rattle sound is produced by a number of hollow rings fixed to the end of the snake's tail. They are joined loosely and rattle when the snake shakes its tail.

Which is the world's fastest reptile?

The world's fastest reptile (measured on land) is the spiny-tailed iguana of Costa Rica.

Iguana

How strong is an alligator's jaw?

Muscles that close the jaws of an alligator are very strong, but once shut, a man can easily hold them closed with his bare hands, though this is not recommended!

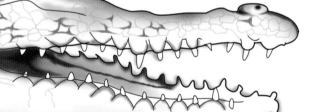

Alligator

What is a gecko?

A gecko is a small insect-eating lizard. It has a large head and a short, stocky body. Geckos are quite common in warm countries, rocky or sandy deserts and semi-arid locations.

Gila Monster

Are lizards poisonous?

There are two types of lizard which are poisonous: the gila monster and the Mexican bearded lizard. They are found in parts of Mexico and the USA.

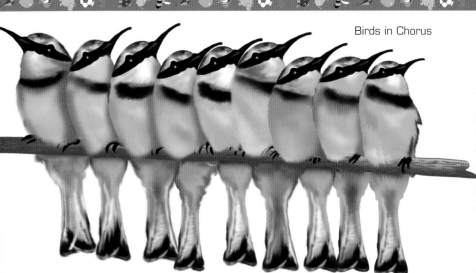

Birds in Chorus

What is a bird?

Birds are a group of warm-blooded vertebrates. These vertebrates fall in the class Aves. They have wings and feathers and are unique from other animals.

Why do birds migrate?

Migration helps birds to have continuous sources of food and water, as well as to avoid environments that are too hot or too cold. Migrating birds use a variety of clues to find their way. These include the position of the sun during the day and the stars at night.

Why do birds sing a dawn chorus?

A dawn chorus is simply each bird proclaiming its right to its territory. The bird warns others not to come too close.

How many species of birds are there?

There are over 10,000 species of birds.

Which bird flies the longest distances to migrate?

The Arctic tern (a small bird) makes the longest migration of any bird. It breeds within the Arctic Circle, but flies to the edge of the Antarctic ice pack during the winter — the total distance roughly being the circumference of the Earth.

Where do budgerigars come from?

A budgerigar is kind of Australian parakeet. The name 'budgerigar' comes from the Australian aborigine language and means 'good cockatoo'. Wild budgies are usually pale green with yellowish heads and brown bars on their wings.

Which is the heaviest flying bird?

The great bustard is the heaviest flying bird in the world, and can weigh up to 20.9 kilograms (46.08 lb).

Which is the biggest eagle in the world?

It is the Harpy eagle, found in the rainforests of South and Central America. Males weigh around 4.54-7.26 kilograms (10-16 lb) and females around 7.26-8.16 kilograms (16-18lb).

Why do woodpeckers peck?

Woodpeckers peck at trees to grab insects on the bark. They also peck to make a noise in the same way that other birds sing.

Woodpeckers

Why do some birds swallow small stones?

Two unusual internal organs help birds to process food. The gizzard, which is part of a bird's stomach, has thick muscular walls with hard inner ridges. It is capable of crushing large seeds and even shellfish. Some seed-eating birds swallow small stones so that the gizzard will grind food more efficiently. Birds that feed on nectar and soft fruit have poorly developed gizzards.

Harpy Eagle

Is it true that lizards squirt blood from their eyes?

Some horned lizards do squirt blood from their eyes as an unusual means of defence. The blood is thought to cause irritation to the enemy's eyes.

What makes the Sumatran rhinoceros different?

The Sumatran rhinoceros is the smallest living rhinoceros. What makes it different is that it has two horns and two deep skin folds encircling the body between legs and trunk. Males' horns are usually larger than those of females.

Horned lizard

How big is a panda when it is born?

When pandas are born, they are smaller than a mouse.

How do hedgehogs protect themselves from enemies?

Hedgehogs have sharp spines on their bodies. In the face of danger their muscles contract to make a spiky ball. A hedgehog can stay like that for a long time.

Hedgehog

What is the colour of the white rhino?

The white rhino isn't white at all. It is grey or dark yellow, depending on the shade of the mud it plays in. The 'white' comes from 'weit', the African word for wide. It is the largest land animal after the elephant.

Kangaroo

Does any bird fly backwards?

The hummingbird is the only bird which can fly backwards. At little over 5.08 centimetres (2 in) from beak tip to tail tip, it is also the smallest bird. Hummingbirds are known for their rapid flight — their strong wing-beat is so rapid that it produces a hum.

What is so funny about the aardvark?

The aardvark is quite odd-looking. It resembles a giant, hump-backed rat with the head of an anteater, the snout of a pig, and the ears of a rabbit. Aardvark is really a Dutch word meaning 'earth pig'.

Aardvark

What is an echidna?

An echidna is a spiny, egg-laying, burrowing animal that lives in Australia and New Guinea. It is a type of anteater and looks like a hedgehog. When attacked it rolls up into a ball.

Why do snakes stare?

Snakes appear to stare simply because they do not have eyelids to cover their eyes. This means that even when resting or hibernating, the snake's eyes are always open.

How do kangaroos use their tail?

Kangaroos run very fast, and they hop and leap while doing so. Their tails help them keep their balance.

Tamarin

Why is the tamarin called 'the golden lion'?

Slightly smaller than squirrels, tamarins are often called 'the golden lion'. The golden lion tamarins have soft silky fur, covering their head and face, which is golden in colour. Their fur resembles the mane of the lion and hence their name.

Which animals sleep the most?

Armadillos, opossums and sloths spend up to 80 percent of their lives sleeping.

How much water does a koala drink?

Koalas do not drink any water at all. Their name means 'no drink'. They get their water from the eucalyptus leaves that they eat.

Which is considered to be the slowest animal?

The three-toed sloth found in South America is said to be the slowest animal in the animal kingdom. It generally covers only 1.83-2.44 metres (6-8 ft) in a minute.

Three-toed Sloth

Which animals are said to form the largest herds?

Springboks travel in large herds. These herds may have thousands of members and may be spread over many kilometres.

How fast can a grizzly bear run?

In spite of being large and heavy, it can run as fast as a horse, about 56 kilometres per hour (35 mph).

Springbok

Why are some animals difficult to spot in their surroundings?

Many animals tend to blend with their surroundings either by changing colour or looking like an object that is a part of the surroundings. This is called a camouflage and is done to avoid being seen by their enemies or their prey.

Which is the largest meat-eating animal on land?

The largest meat-eating animal on land is the polar bear.

Which is considered to be the smallest mammal?

The pygmy shrew found in South Africa is about 5.08 centimetres (2 in) long and weighs about 1.2- 2.7 grams (0.042- 0.095 oz).

Which is the world's biggest lizard?

Found in Indonesia, the komodo dragon is the world's biggest lizard and a fierce predator. It can kill a 45.36 kilograms (100 lb) wild boar and eat it in one sitting. It can run fast, can climb trees and also swim!

Which is the only animal that can swim, climb trees and stand as well as sit upright?

A bear is the only animal that can climb trees, swim, stand and sit upright.

Komodo dragon

life in the oceans

Where did life first evolve?

Life first evolved in water. About 70 percent of the earth's surface is covered by oceans, which are the largest water bodies. More than 95 percent of the water on Earth had a high salt content that made it suitable for life to evolve.

Where is life found in the oceans?

Oceans can be divided into three zones, where different creatures are found, depending upon how much sunlight they receive. The shallow zone that receives the most sunlight is called the Sunlit Zone. The zone that gets only a small amount of light is called the Twilight Zone. The deep waters where sunlight cannot reach is called the Midnight Zone.

What does marine life mean?

Life that is found in seas or oceans is called marine life. It is a colourful world of different varieties of fish, plants, corals, dolphins, whales and other sea creatures.

Are there any plants in the seas?

There are some tiny plants that float in the sea in groups. These are called plankton. They are so small that they cannot be seen with our naked eyes. They are a source of food for fish and other sea creatures — even whales.

Sunlit Zone

Plants like plankton and fish of many colours and shapes are found in the Sunlit Zone.

Twilight Zone

Lantern fish, rat-tail fish, hatchet fish and mid-water jellyfish are found in the Twilight Zone.

Midnight Zone

Other varieties of fish, anemones, oysters and squids are found in the Midnight Zone.

12

Flying Fish

What are flying fish?

A flying fish is a small fish that can glide through the air for several hundred metres.
It is a small fish that can swim rapidly through water, moving its tail vigorously. It spreads its fins to move. The fast speed at which it moves helps to lift the fish above the water.

Do fish feel the cold?

No, fish do not feel the cold. They are 'cold-blooded' organisms — their body temperature changes according to the temperature outside. So if it is cold outside, their temperature is low, if it is hot outside then their temperature is high.

Is the jellyfish a fish?

No, the jellyfish is not a fish. It is a kind of plankton without a skeleton. Nine-tenths of the body of a jellyfish is made of a squishy jelly-like substance. It does not have a brain or blood. For a stomach, it just has a hollow space!

What are fish?

Fish are creatures found in water, which do not have a backbone or limbs. They have fins to help them swim in water and gills to breathe.

How do fish breathe?

First, the fish takes water into its mouth. The water is forced over the gills inside the fish and out through the gill slits. The fish have these slits on each side of the back part of the head. Blood vessels in the gills take oxygen from the water and the blood then carries it around the body.

Can any fish live without water?

There are some fish that spend quite some time out of the water. Their gills have adapted to breathe in air for some time. The flying fish and the climbing perch are fish that can stay out of water for some time.

Do fish sleep?

By 'sleep' we usually mean a period of rest when the eyes are closed and there is no movement. But most fish do not have eyelids except for sharks! There are fish that never stop moving and yet there are some that hardly move at all! Some are active by day and some are active by night. So we cannot be sure whether they sleep, rest or not.

Where did the goldfish come from?

The ancestor of the goldfish is the carp that is found in the lakes and rivers of China and Japan. The Chinese and Japanese have been breeding goldfish for many years. Goldfish were first brought to Europe about 200 years ago. They were first given to Madame Pompadour of the court of King Louis XV of France.

Goldfish

Which is the world's largest fish?

The whale shark is the world's largest fish. It grows to more than 50 feet in length and may weigh several tons. It lives in the warm parts of the Atlantic, the Pacific and Indian Oceans.

Tiny Gobi

What is a piranha?

The piranha is a fish that lives in the rivers of South America. It is particularly famous for its greediness. Four of the dozen or so species of piranha fish are dangerous.

Do the Japanese eat poisonous fish?

The Japanese eat the puffer fish as a delicacy. It is a fish that has poison in some of its organs such as the heart and the liver. But Japanese chefs are specially trained to cook it in such a way that it loses its poison!

Which is the world's smallest fish?

The tiny goby found in Luzon, Philippines, is the world's smallest fish. It rarely grows longer than 1.27 centimetres (0.5 in).

13

Which is the oldest class of fish?

Lampreys and hagfish are the earliest fish. They are primitive and fish-like animals, with no jaws and skeletons. They have smooth skin without any scales. These fish are found near the sea bottom.

How do puffer fish puff themselves up?

All puffer fish puff themselves up by pumping water into special sacks. When they are out of water these sacks fill with air and they take on a balloon-like appearance.

Can any fish climb trees?

Climbing perch are fish that can climb trees. They are found in the Far East. They can cross land by spreading rows of thorn-like spines on their gill covers.

How did the catfish get its name?

The catfish has feelers on its mouth that look like a cat's whiskers. These feelers help the catfish sense its surroundings. When this fish is caught it makes a buzzing or croaking sound, which is similar to a cat's purring. That is how it got its name.

How do scientists classify fish?

Scientists classify fish into two main groups —fish without jaws (hagfish and lampreys) and fish with jaws. The fish with jaws are further divided into those with skeletons made of cartilage (sharks, chimaeras, skates and rays) and those with bony skeletons (herring, cod, flounders and barracudas).

How fast can tuna swim?

Tuna can reach 80 kilometres per hour (50 mph) in short bursts. Some of them can swim for long stretches and make it up to 8-16 kilometres per hour (5- 10 mph).

What is a cuttlefish?

The cuttlefish is not a fish but a creature with a shell. It moves in water smoothly and silently using its row of fins. It has a strong shield-shaped body. On seeing prey, it shoots out its tentacles from the pockets that are located in its broad head behind its bulging eyes.

What is strange about the flatfishes' eyes?

Four families of flatfish (tongue soles and turbots) always have eyes on the left side and two groups of flatfish (both flounders) have eyes on the right side.

How are sardines canned?

The sardines are caught when they are small. They are put in bins filled with fresh water. They are cleaned and scaled and the heads are removed. Then they are dipped in salt and poured into large trays that are passed under an artificial drier. Finally, they are cooked for about five minutes in boiling oil. After they have been cooled, they are put in cans and further soaked in oil to keep them moist.

Which fish give out light?

Many fish live in the deep waters of the ocean where no light reaches. So, some fish give out light to signal to other fish or creatures. The lantern fish is one such fish that has a row of lights along its body. The angler fish swims around with a lighted rod that attracts other fish which are then swallowed by it.

Climbing Perch   Cuttle Fish   Angler Fish

What are sharks?

Sharks are fish with jaws and slits in the skin to breathe. They also have a backbone. The shark's mouth is located on the underside of its head. It rolls over on its back to get its food on the surface. Sharks may be as big as 0.3 metres to 15 metres.

Is the blue shark really blue?

The blue shark shows a bright blue colour on the upper part of its body and is white underneath. The blue quickly fades to dull grey after the shark is killed. Most sharks are brown, olive or grayish.

Which shark is found in freshwater?

The bull shark is the only shark that can live in fresh water. It prefers to live in shallow coastal waters. It commonly enters bays, lagoons and river mouths.

Why are the tiger shark and the great white shark dangerous?

The tiger shark lives in tropical waters and may be as big as 270 kilograms (595 lb). It can swallow a sea lion and has been known to attack human beings. The great white shark may be 12 metres (39 ft) in length and is known to eat human beings and sea lions in one gulp!

Why do stingrays sting?

Stingrays only sting if you step on them, otherwise they can be fed by hand and petted! They have a poison filled spine at the end of their tail, which produces the sting effect.

Stingray

What are rays and skates?

Shark

Rays and skates belong to the shark family. Rays are big fish that can weigh more than a ton and be more than 6 metres (20 ft) wide! They live in warm waters. While the skates are similar and have a pancake-shaped body, they are not as large or heavy as the rays. The skates are groundfish that lie buried in sand or gravel on the sea bottom. They swim very slowly unless disturbed.

Electric Ray

What is an electric ray?

An electric ray is a fish that can give powerful electric shocks to anyone who touches it.

Do all sharks eat people?

Of the 150 species of sharks, most are harmless! There are two species of sharks that are quite dangerous — the 'Tiger Shark' and the 'Great White Shark'. These may, at times, eat people.

Why do jellyfish sting?

Jellyfish use their tentacles to sting. They capture smaller creatures for food by stinging and paralysing them. Some jellyfish also have stinging organs in the stomach to destroy the prey completely.

What attracts sharks?

Scientists are still not sure of what attracts sharks. Sometimes sounds like those made by a swimmer or a fish attract sharks. Yellow, white and silver colours attract some sharks. Though blood alone does not attract them, a combination of colour, smell and sound may invite an attack.

Which shark is found in freshwater?

The bull shark is the only shark that can live in fresh water. It prefers to live in shallow coastal waters. It commonly enters bays, lagoons and river mouths.

Which is the biggest shark of all?

The biggest shark is the whale shark. It may grow up to 15 metres (49 ft) in length and weigh 18 tonnes but it is completely harmless. It mainly feeds on plankton.

Whale Shark

sea mammals - whales, dolphins & porpoises

Where are sea mammals found in the seas?

Sea mammals are found near the ocean surface where it is easier for them to breathe. They may go deeper to search for food but they need to come up frequently.

Dolphin

How can you tell the difference between a dolphin and a porpoise?

The easiest way to tell the difference is to look at the head. Dolphins appear to have a beak, whereas the head of the porpoise is rounded.

Porpoise

What is a porpoise?

A porpoise is a sea mammal that also breathes through the blow-hole and feeds its young with milk. Its tail is horizontal and not at a right angle like the tails of fish. From a distance it looks like a dolphin.

Who was Pelorus Jack?

Pelorus Jack was the name of a porpoise that guided ships through an area of dangerous sea near New Zealand from 1871 to 1912. The waters had many dangerous currents and hidden rocks, but by following Jack, the ships were able to navigate the channel safely. The porpoise was called Pelorus Jack as the ships sailed from Pelorus Sound.

Why do whales have holes at the top of their heads?

Whales have nostrils or blow-holes at the top of their heads to breathe. They swim to the surface to throw out used air from their lungs. They make a loud sound while breathing that may be heard over a distance. Whales rise to the surface to breathe every five or ten minutes, but they can remain under water for about 45 minutes!

What is a killer whale?

Killer whales are very intelligent and friendly animals. They work in groups when they hunt. They also come to the beach temporarily when they have to catch their favourite food — sea lions.

What is a manatee?

A manatee is an animal of the sea-cow family. It is believed that these creatures inspired the legendary stories of mermaids.

How do whales keep warm?

Whales have a layer of fat called blubber that keeps them warm in cold weather and low temperatures.

Why are whales different from other fish?

Whales are mammals and not fish. They give birth to their young ones and feed them with their milk. They are warm-blooded creatures. They have lungs to breathe instead of gills.

What is a dugong?

Dugongs are animals closely related to manatees found in the coastal waters of East Africa, the Red Sea, the Malay Peninsula and others. They are pale cream in colour but darken with age to a deep slate gray. They have short hair lightly covering their bodies and a thick and tough skin.

Are dolphins fishes?

No, dolphins are sea mammals. They have lungs to breathe and they give birth to their young ones, unlike fish, which lay eggs.

Manatee

What is the humpback whale famous for?

The humpback whales are best known for their songs that can be heard hundreds of miles under the sea.

Killer Whale

How long can sea turtles stay under water?

Sea turtles must swim to the ocean surface to breathe every few minutes. When they are resting, they can remain under water for more than an hour without breathing.

Turtle

How does a turtle come out of its shell?

Turtles have only one shell but it is divided into two parts — one covers the back, the other covers the underside of the turtle's body. It can force out its head, neck, tail and legs through the openings between the two parts of the shell.

What is the Kemps Ridley turtle?

The Kemps Ridley turtle is the rarest of all sea turtles. It weighs between 36-45 kilograms (80-100 lb) and is of an olive green colour. They nest in large numbers and are found near a single beach near Rancho Nuevo in Mexico.

What are hooded seals?

The hooded seal is a large member of the hair seal family. They are found in the North Atlantic Ocean. These seals are large and fierce-looking. They have dark black blotches on a grey background.

What is the difference between a turtle and a tortoise?

Turtles and tortoises are both four-legged reptiles. They have hard outer shells, scaly skin, horny beaks and short legs. A turtle is a sea reptile whereas the tortoise is a land reptile.

What are the different types of seals and where do they live?

Seals can be of various types — fur seals, sea lions, hair seals, sea elephants and the walrus. They are mammals that have descended from land mammals. They cannot live under water all the time. Their young ones are born on land and are taught to swim by their mothers.

Why do walruses have tusks?

A walrus can have a tusk, 100 centimetres (39 in) in size for a male or 80 centimetres (31 in) in size for a female. The tusks are used by the male to attract the female walrus. Tusks are rarely used as weapons, but they help a walrus get on to the ice floor.

Which is the world's biggest turtle?

The leatherback is the world's biggest turtle. It usually weighs about 450 kilograms (992 lb) and the biggest specimen on record is over 2 metres (7 ft) long and weighing 680 kilograms (1500 lb).

How do you tell the difference between seals and sea lions?

Sea lions and fur seals have small flap like ears on the outside whereas seals have tiny ear holes. Sea lions have flippers that are like wings whereas seals have short and blunt flippers. Lastly, sea lions do not have flippers with nails but seals have claw-like nails.

Which seals are in danger of disappearing?

The Hawaiian monk seals are in danger of disappearing altogether and need to be saved. Caribbean monk seals are becoming rare too. For too long, men have hunted them for their own benefit leaving just a few alive today.

Sea Lion

How is coral formed?

Coral is made up of the skeletons of small sea creatures that have shells formed out of limestone. Corals are of many shapes and colours. They live in large colonies, which build up over time to form coral reefs.

What is the Bentooth bristlemouth?

This is a type of small fish that produces light because of tiny organs arranged along its underbelly. It is a common fish found in oceans.

Does a starfish have eyes?

Starfish have eyes at the tips of their arms! These eyes are protected by a circle of spines.

Why are reefs called the 'rainforests of the sea'?

Coral reefs are rich in diverse varieties of animal and plant life. Many types of small, beautiful fish and sea slugs, colourful sea anemones, sea urchins and starfish live in the reefs.

Which anemone stings?

The carpet anemone can sting using its short tentacles. Its sting causes an uncomfortable rash on unprotected skin. It uses its stinging cells to capture fish.

What is a sponge?

The dried colourless sponge used in our kitchens and bathrooms is not a real sponge. It looks like a real sponge but is made of synthetic material. Real sponges are found in the sea and are the most primitive sea animals. They breathe and feed themselves through their pores.

How many types of starfish are there?

Starfish can be of three types. The brittle stars break off their long snaky rays when caught. Their arms may extend from 20 to 25 centimetres (8-10 in). There are the feather stars whose rays look like little plumes, and the ordinary sea stars which measure about 13 centimetres (5 in).

Which sea creatures can be dangerous to divers?

Moray eels, octopuses, sea urchins with sharp spines, jelly fish, stingrays and toad fish can attack divers. The carpet anemone and the Portugese man-of-war are also known to cause a rash.

What are starfish?

Starfish are small fish with star shaped bodies and a central mouth. Their tough, leathery skin is covered with short spines. On the upper and undersides, they have button-shaped discs located in the centre. They take in and throw out water through these discs. They use their arms to move and smell and they have grooves and tube-like feet to help them move.

Where is the red cauliflower coral found?

The red cauliflower coral is a beautiful soft coral found in the Indo-Pacific region. It has a flowery shape and ranges from bright red to deep orange. It feeds at night and contracts into a tight ball by day.

How strong is an attack by the mantis shrimp?

The mantis shrimp can break the glass of an aquarium or split a human thumb to the bone with one strike!

What is strange about the harlequin shrimp's food?

The harlequin shrimp is a colourful shrimp with bright spots all over. It blends with the background completely. It eats only starfish for food. It flips the starfish over and feeds on its soft underside.

How many types of jellyfish are there?

Jellyfish may be very tiny or as big as 0.5 metres in diameter. They are of different shapes and colours, some of which seem to glow when they are disturbed. Most jellyfish live on or near the water surface, but there are a few which live near the bottom of the sea.

What are molluscs?

Molluscs are a group of animals without backbones. They include snails, clams, oysters and octopuses. They vary in size from being invisible to as big as 15 metres (49 ft) long. Molluscs have soft, slimy bodies that are boneless and are covered with big folds of flesh called 'mantles'. They have a 'foot' that is an extension of the mantle and helps them move. All mollusks lay eggs.

Where does the red hermit crab get its name?

The red hermit crab is so called because it carries its home around on its back like a hermit! Since it has a soft and vulnerable abdomen, it uses discarded snail shells for protection. As it grows, it looks for larger shells to hide itself!

What are barnacles?

A barnacle is a small shellfish. When barnacles are hatched they swim freely but when they grow up they cannot move about. Then they attach themselves to any surface like piers, rocks, wood or iron.

What are snails?

Snails are molluscs and can be of two types. Some snails have shells and some are covered by a thin mantle and are called slugs. All snails have a large foot on the underside; that is why they are also called stomach feet. They breathe with a single lung or gill.

Why do clams close up their shells?

If the clam gets a shock and its shell is open, it stretches its neck outside and squirts out water or it pulls in its neck and closes its shell hurriedly.

Can crabs attack?

Crabs are known for their hard shells that they remove and discard when they grow. While the new shell takes time to harden, they are vulnerable to predators. During this stage, some crabs may use their claws to exert hundreds of pounds of pressure to save themselves. Some can produce a miniature sound boom that can deafen or stun their prey.

Are there any poisonous snails?

Some snails like the cone shells produce toxic venom. These are found in tropical regions. They inject poison through a spear-shaped rod.

What is a 'tomalley'?

Tomalley is the lobster's liver that is green in colour but turns red on cooking. It is considered a delicacy in some countries.

How do crayfish, shrimps and prawns differ?

The prawn of Great Britain is called the shrimp in the United States. The only difference is that the second flap on the abdomen of the prawns overlaps the first and the third one. The crayfish or crawfish are names given both to a common fresh water animal with a shell and to a spiny lobster found in salty water.

What is a squid?

A squid has a long, slender body with triangular fins at its edges. It has a short square head and well-developed eyes and 10 arms. Two of its tentacles are longer and more flexible than others. These are used to capture the prey; the others are used to transfer food to the mouth. The squid can also discharge an ink-like fluid to hide itself.

How do lobsters grow?

All through their lives, lobsters molt. They shed their shell whenever they outgrow it. During the first year, they molt fourteen to seventeen times but when they grow older they do not molt more than once a year.

Do lobsters have teeth?

Lobsters have teeth in their stomach. The stomach is near the mouth and the food is actually chewed in the stomach between three grinding surfaces that are called the 'gastric mill'.

How does an octopus save itself from its enemies?

When an enemy approaches, the octopus throws a 'smoke screen' and escapes. It can throw a black ink-like fluid that clouds the surrounding water.
An octopus can also change its colour from red to grey, yellow, brown or sea green to match its surroundings.

What is an octopus?

An octopus is an animal with eight tentacles that are long and flexible, thus its name 'octopus'. These tentacles help in gathering its prey.

How does an octopus move?

The octopus has a funnel in its back part. It shoots a stream of water with force from it and moves itself backwards rapidly.

How do oysters produce pearls?

When a foreign substance like a grain of sand sticks into the shell of the oyster, its body reacts to it by depositing layers of pearl-like substance around it. The foreign body gets covered in layers and this is what we call a pearl.

Do squids give off light?

Some squids give off light. They have light organs on the mantle, the arms, inside the mantle and around their eyes. At night, they appear beautiful as they glow.

What are seaworms?

Seaworms look like the common earthworm. One of the more interesting varieties is the tube worm. These animals form a hard-shelled tube that provides them protection.

What is a sea horse?

The sea horse is a fish that has a head shaped like a pony. Solid plates and thorny spikes cover its body. Its tail is like a snake's, which it curls around a bit of seaweed so that it does not get carried away by the water. It swims with a single fin on its back and it moves upright through the water. Its mouth is like a pipe, which is used to suck in food.

What is special about the giant squid?

The giant squid is the largest animal without a backbone on this earth. Some giant squids found in the North Atlantic have been found to measure a length of 16 metres (53 ft).

Which is the biggest clam caught and eaten in the United States?

The Geoduck clam caught in the North-west Pacific Ocean weighs an average of 1.3 kilograms (3 lb) and yields over 500 grams (1 lb) of meat.

How do sea horses take care of their young ones?

The female sea horse lays her eggs and puts them into the broad pouch beneath the tail of the male. The father then carries the eggs until they hatch. Even after they hatch, they remain in the father's pouch till they are able to take care of themselves.

How much electricity does an electric eel produce?

The average electricity that an electric eel produces is more than 350 volts but it can even produce as much as 650 volts.

What is a coconut crab?

A coconut crab is a large hermit crab that lives on tropical Pacific Islands. The crab gets its name because it eats coconut and has even been caught on coconuts. These crabs are considered a delicacy on the island.

Do octopuses have intelligence?

Octopuses are intelligent animals and have the ability to learn. An octopus at London Zoo in England learned how to twist the lid of a jar to reach a crab inside!

Moray Eel

What are moray eels?

Moray eels are different from common eels because they do not have side fins but have well-developed teeth. They are found in tropical and subtropical waters. They can swim (unlike other fish) backwards.

What are 'milky seas'?

Living creatures like bacteria, jellyfish and others sometimes give off light. This makes a certain part of the sea glow; for example, the water in the Western Arabian Sea usually glows because of bacteria that emit light. This occurrence is called 'milky seas.'

What are insects?

Insects are creepy-crawly creatures with three pairs of legs, and a pair of antennae on the front of the head. Some insects are very colourful and beautiful; others are ugly-looking and scary.

How many varieties of insects are there in the world?

There are over 1 million varieties of insects in the world, and some estimate that there might be as many as 10 million.

How do insects breathe?

Insects breathe through holes (spiracles) on the sides of their body.

Head

Antennae

How useful are insects?

Insects produce honey, silk, wax and other products for us. They also help in the growth of plants and crops through pollination, help clear muck and are food for other creatures. But insects are major pests too as they destroy crops and spread diseases. However, less than one percent of insect species are pests.

What are the main body parts of an insect?

All insects have three pairs of legs. Their body is divided into three main parts: head, abdomen and thorax. The head has a pair of feelers or antennae on its front. The thorax has 6 legs and a pair of wings.

Wings

Abdomen

Leg

What is unusual about an insect's eyes?

Most insects have two compound eyes. Some insects have three simple eyes on the top of their heads in addition to the compound eyes. Their unusual eyes give them 360 degree wrap-around vision. This means they don't have to turn their heads to see behind them. They can see colours. With their compound eyes, they can also react faster to moving images.

What kinds of habitat do insects live in?

Insects are marvellous creatures. They can live anywhere — jungles, deserts, hot regions, freezing climates. The only places where insects are not commonly found are the oceans.

What do the antennae do for the insects?

Insects can smell and touch with their antennae. An insect called a moth, which has feather-like antennae, can spot another moth miles away. The long antennae of cockroaches help them feel their way in the dark.

How do insects fly?

The insects wings are very thin and the insect must flap them very fast to fly. Insects can twist and turn their wings, so that they stay in one spot in the air or even fly backwards.

Do all insects fly?

Many insects can fly; some cannot. Flying insects have one or two pairs of wings. Butterflies, moths, dragonflies, mosquitoes and common flies are some of the well-known flying insects. Some insects like springtails, fleas and lice cannot fly.

Which is the longest insect?

The longest insect is a 'stick bug' from the rain forests of Borneo. The largest specimen ever recorded is in the Natural History Museum in London. Its body length is 32.77 centimetres (12.9 in). Its total length, including its legs, is 50.80 centimetres (20 in)!

Which is the heaviest insect?

The goliath beetle is the world's heaviest insect. It can weigh up to 100 grams (3.53 oz).

Which is the fastest running insect?

The fastest running insect is the Australian tiger beetle, which can run almost 9.01 kilometres per hour (5.6 mph) .

Which is the smallest insect?

Fairy fly wasps are the smallest insects.They are only 0.2 millimetres ($1/100$ in) long.

Which were the first insects with wings?

The first insects with wings were dragonflies. The meganeura was a huge dragonfly with a wing span of about 75 centimetres (29.53 in).

Which is the loudest insect?

The loudest insects are cicadas, which can be heard up to 400 metres (1,312 ft) away.

Which insect migrates over the longest distance?

The desert locust migrates from the west coast of Africa to islands in the West Indies and back each year — some 4500 kilometres (2796.17 miles) each way!

Which is the largest insect?

The acteon beetle from South America is considered to be the largest known insect in the world. The male of this species can be 9 centimetres long, (3.54 in) 5 centimetres (1.97 in) wide and 4 centimetres (1.54 in) thick.

Which is the largest moth?

The largest moth is the Asian Atlas moth, which can be as long as 33.02 centimetres (13 in) from its front wing tip to rear wing tip.

Which is the fastest flying insect?

The fastest flying insect is the dragonfly. It has been recorded flying at 157.72 kilometres per hour (98 mph). It can catch up with your motor car, quite comfortably!

beware of these

American Cockroach

How friendly are houseflies?

Houseflies are believed to transmit more than 200 different parasites and pathogens to humans

Which is the most dangerous ant?

The black bulldog ant of Australia stings and bites at the same time and has been known to cause death in humans.

Velvet Ant

Why do bees have stings?

Stings help bees protect their hives. They usually sting only if they have to since most bees die soon after they sting. Honeybees have little hooks at the end of their stings.

When a honeybee stings, the sting gets stuck in the victim's skin and gets pulled out, thus killing the bee.

Are cockroaches harmful?

Although cockroaches don't produce any poisonous secretions, they carry human dirt and germs around.

Which insect poisons its victims using its spines?

The hollow spines of the caterpillar break as soon as they touch the victim's skin, thus allowing toxins contained in the spines to flow into the wound, causing a lot of pain.

Which is the most poisonous insect?

The mutilid wasp, a South African velvet ant, is the most poisonous insect in the world.

Which insect has the worst sting?

The tarantula hawk, an insect found in North America, has the severest and the most painful sting.

Which is the most dangerous insect in the world?

The anopheles mosquito is considered to be the most dangerous insect in the world. It's said to be responsible for about 270 million cases of malaria and 2 million deaths in 1990.

Anopheles Mosquito

Which insects can sting more than once?

Wasps, yellow jackets and hornets have a lance-like sting without barbs and can sting repeatedly.

What happens when you get stung by an insect?

When stung by an insect like a wasp or a bee, you will feel some pain and discomfort, while some insect bites like that of a mosquito will leave behind an itching sensation. The skin around the bite usually turns red and swells, but will be fine after sometime even if it is not treated.

Hornet

Are bees our friends?

Bees collect nectar from flowers, which we get as honey. As they visit a variety of plants to collect nectar, in the process they pollinate fruits, vegetables and crops, and thus help in their growth.

Honey bee

What is beeswax?

Honeybees secrete beeswax in their abdomens. Bees have to eat two to four pounds of honey to produce one pound of beeswax. Humans use this beeswax extensively — in making candles, crayons, inks, lipsticks, creams, lotions and other products.

Frog Beetle

What are fireflies?

Fireflies are insects which glow in the dark. They are also called glow worms. Hundreds of fireflies flying around together at night are a fascinating sight — like twinkling stars within a hand's reach.

From which insect do you get a red dye?

An insect called the cochineal is an excellent source of natural red dye. These insects are dried and ground into a powder and then cooked to release the maximum amount of colour. This dye is used to colour fabric and basketry materials.

Why are ladybirds considered gardener's friends?

Because they eat aphids, which are harmful to many plants in the garden.

Is a frog beetle a frog or a beetle?

The frog beetle is an incredibly colourful beetle in metallic green with a cerise and gold coloured band down its back. Its thick legs are set back in its body like those of a frog. Hence the name.

Can you eat insects?

Yes, insects like beetles, moths and ants and some types of insect larvae are used as food in many regions.

Why do children love butterflies?

The beautiful colours of butterflies fascinate little children. They run after the butterflies, trying to catch them as they hop from flower to flower, and enjoy all the fun.

How are silk moths useful to us?

Silk moths give us silk. Silkworm caterpillars feed on mulberry leaves. After they form pupae, the cocoons are collected and boiled to release the silk fibres. These long stranded fibres are collected and spun into thread and, in turn, the thread is woven into silk fabrics, which give us beautiful clothes. Each cocoon produces a thread of silk that may be over 1 kilometre (0.6 miles) long!

Silk moth

all about butterflies

How many eggs does a butterfly lay?

Butterflies can lay hundreds of eggs, either one at a time or in clusters.

What is a butterfly's life cycle?

A butterfly's life cycle includes four stages: egg, caterpillar (or larva), pupa and adult. An adult female lays eggs, often on the undersides of leaves. The eggs hatch into tiny larvae (caterpillar). Caterpillars eat and grow quickly. They then attach themselves to twigs and form a hard outer shell called the pupa. Inside the pupa the caterpillar transforms into a butterfly.

What do butterflies eat?

Adult butterflies sip nectar from flowers through their tongues, which they use like straws. Some butterflies do not visit flowers, but feed on tree sap or rotting organic material.

Which butterfly has the longest lifespan?

The Mourning Cloak and Compton Tortoiseshell are Canadian butterflies with the longest life span. They can live for up to 11 months.

Where do butterflies live in winter?

They migrate to warmer climates like Australia, South America and Africa.

Life Cycle of a Butterfly

Which are the largest and the smallest butterflies?

The Queen Alexandra's Birdwing is the largest, with a wing span of 280 millimetres (11^1/$_8$ in). It is found in the rain forests of New Guinea. The smallest is the pygmy blue found in the United States. Its wingspan is 15 millimetres (^{1}/$_2$ in).

What are spire butterflies?

Spire butterflies look much like Monarch butterflies except that their colours are more vivid — pink, yellow, cyan and turquoise green. They change colour according to their mood. They are usually found in great flocks, which dance about the skies like giant multi-coloured clouds.

How do caterpillars turn into a butterfly?

Butterfly caterpillars can spin thread from their mouths. They use this to bind leaves together for a shelter, which is the cocoon. Inside the cocoon, the caterpillar transforms into a butterfly.

What is the difference between a butterfly and a moth?

Why do butterflies fly on warm summer days?

Butterflies are creatures of the sun and fly best when they're warm. On a warm summer's day, butterflies flutter from flower to flower feeding on nectar. On cool days, they perch on rocks or bask in the sun to absorb heat.

A butterfly can fold its wings, while a moth always keeps them spread. They are also distinguished by the shape of the antennae. Butterfly antennae are long and thread-like, with a small knob at the end. Moth antennae are thread-like or feather-like.

Bee-hive

Which insects build permanent homes?

Bees, wasps and ants are the only insects that build permanent homes.

Where do bumblebees live?

Bumblebees are big, fuzzy insects, which everyone can recognise by their robust shape and black and yellow colouration. They live in colonies and build their small nests in holes or cracks in the ground. Compared with honeybees, only a few hundred of them live in a single nest.

Bumblebee

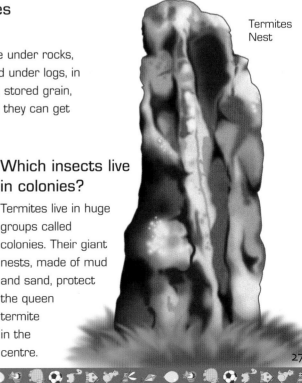

Where do bees live?

Bees normally build their nests in the soil but they may use other natural holes such as abandoned rodent nests or tree hollows. Honeybees are the only insects which live in hives, which they build using beeswax. Honeybees live in colonies with a single queen and many workers. Each honeybee colony can have 50,000 to 60,000 workers.

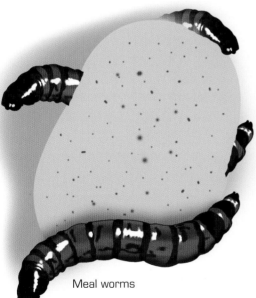

Meal worms

What are common wasps' nests made of?

Common wasps build their nests from chewed-up wood fibre.

Which insect lives under rocks?

Mealworms usually live under rocks, but they are also found under logs, in animal burrows and in stored grain, mostly in areas where they can get enough food.

Which insects make their nests from mud?

Mud daubers build clay or mud-cell nests.

Termites Nest

How do cicada killers build their homes?

Cicada killers dig homes about one half inch across and pile the excavated soil around the opening.

Where is the milkweed bug found?

Milkweed bugs can be usually found in small groups on milkweed plants, often on the underside of the leaves.

What kind of nests do hornets live in?

Hornets and yellow jackets build football-shaped paper-like nests to live in.

Which insects live in colonies?

Termites live in huge groups called colonies. Their giant nests, made of mud and sand, protect the queen termite in the centre.

27

aquatic insects

What are aquatic insects?

Aquatic insects live most of their lives in water.

What is a 'water tiger'?

The 'water tiger' is the larva of the diving beetle. The adult and larvae of this beetle prey upon aquatic insects, fish, and other small animals!

Diving Beetle

How do backswimmers swim?

Backswimmers swim upside-down on their backs just under the surface of the water. They swim by moving their long hind legs like the oars of a boat.

Water Strider

Which insects skate on water?

Water striders skate along the surface of ponds. Their modified leg tips prevent these insects from breaking the water's surface tension.

How do dragonflies and damselflies capture their prey?

Dragonflies and damselflies have a unique way of capturing their prey. They fold their long, bristly legs into a basket or a netlike shape beneath their bodies during the flight. Then, they almost scoop their prey right out of the air! Once the prey is caught, they use their legs to quickly transfer it from the 'trap' to their mouth.

What is unusual about the mayfly?

The mayfly larvae live underwater and can live up to two years. However, as an adult it has the shortest lifespan of all insects — a few hours or, at times, a couple of days. They emerge suddenly in huge numbers from lakes and rivers, piling up along the shores or nearby roads.

Mayfly

Do beetles swim?

Beetles are often seen swimming or crawling among water plants or in the bottom of shallow pools. Their hind legs move alternately when swimming.

What are 'electric light bugs'?

Giant water bugs at times leave the water and fly for the streetlights. Hence, they are also known as 'electric light bugs'.

Which beetles are the strongest swimmers?

Whirligig beetles are strong surface swimmers. Their eyes are divided horizontally — the upper part helps them see above the water while the lower part of their eyes is specialised for underwater viewing.

How do aquatic insects breathe underwater?

Insects, when they live underwater as larvae, have gills to breathe. Some insects like giant water bugs and water scorpions breathe through tubes that reach to the surface of the water. The diving beetle actually carries a bubble of air as it swims underwater.

Where are water boatmen found?

They are usually found at the bottom of shallow ponds, lakes, or roadside ditches, where they swim rapidly and feed on algae or dead organic matter.

Water Boatman

Which butterfly effectively uses its resemblance to the Monarch butterfly to protect itself from predators?

The Viceroy has evolved a striking resemblance to the beautiful but foul-tasting Monarch. The two are so similar that predators — mainly birds — avoid the Viceroy. The Viceroy is not foul-tasting, but has benefited from the unpleasant reputation of the Monarch.

How does the stick insect camouflage itself?

Stick insects are masters of the art of camouflage. They blend into a whole range of backgrounds from bark to leaves and always end up looking like a stick.

Which caterpillar disguises itself as a twig?

The caterpillar we know as an 'inch worm' imitates a twig and can even remain motionless for a long time.

Katydids

Which insect has perfected the hiding trick?

Katydids — they are nocturnal insects, and they use their cryptic colouration to remain unnoticed during the day when they are inactive. They remain perfectly still. Katydids have perfected the hiding trick so well that their body colouring and shape matches that of leaves (including half eaten leaves, dying leaves and leaves with bird droppings), sticks, twigs and tree bark.

Longhorn Beetle

Which beetle disguises itself as a wasp?

The longhorn beetle has black and orange stripes that make it look like a wasp, but it's really a beetle that can't sting at all.

Which insect is camouflaged as an orchid flower?

The orchid mantis is camouflaged as an orchid flower and hence its name.

How does the leaf insect hide?

The leaf insect, as its name suggests, 'hides' from its enemies by resembling leaf veins, a leaf damage caused by insects or fungi, or a leaf trembling in the wind.

How do butterflies protect themselves from predators?

The bright colours of butterflies blend so well with their habitat that it becomes difficult for a predator to find them. Moreover, their colours distract the attacker. The beautiful Indian dead-leaf butterfly seemingly disappears on being approached by its predators — it closes its wings and looks like a dead leaf.

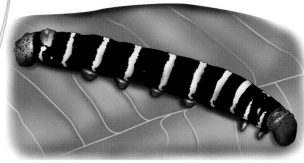

Which insect keeps its predators away because its colours resemble that of a snake?

The Frangipani Sphinx moth has black, red, and yellow colouring similar to that of the deadly coral snake. This keeps a lot of predators away.

Which bug has many ways to scare predators?

Peanut Head Bug

If being ugly isn't enough to scare predators away, the peanut head bug has a full assortment of defences. It can blend in with the bark of a tree to hide. If that does not work, it opens its wings, which have two big spots on the back that look like an owl's eyes, which could scare a small bird away or at least startle it, giving the bug time to escape.

29

How do ladybirds protect themselves?

Ladybirds bleed to protect themselves. When alarmed, they release drops of a reddish or yellowish bitter-tasting liquid from their mouths and from the pores at their joints. This repels prospective attackers.

Dancing bee

Do insects fight?

Of course! When a queen bee is ready to start a new hive, she lays several queen bee larvae. When they hatch there is a great battle, and the strongest one wins.

How do crickets chirp?

Crickets don't chirp from their mouths. They make all that noise by rubbing their wings together.

Cricket

How does the bombardier beetle defend itself?

The bombardier beetle defends itself by firing a boiling hot spray from the rear of its abdomen. The spray is formed by the mixing of chemicals from two glands in the beetle's abdomen. The spray changes instantly into a gas as it is directed away from the beetle. The gas irritates the eyes of the enemy and forms a smoke screen, which helps the beetle escape.

Bombardier Beetle

Why do bees dance?

A worker bee dances to let the other bees know that nectar has been found. The speed, angle and the shape of the dance combined tell the bees about the exact location of the nectar.

Which insect has ears in its legs?

Katydids have ears in their front legs.

How fertile are queen termites?

Queen termites can lay one egg per second for more than 14 years. This gives a total of more than 440,000,000 babies from one queen!

Do insects migrate?

Monarch butterflies migrate thousands of miles between Canada or the Northern United States and Mexico each winter!

Ants

Can insects lift any weight?

Ants can lift 50 times their own weight. But that's nothing compared to the honeybee, which can lift 300 times its own weight — roughly the equivalent of a person lifting 15 tons!

Which human behaviour do ants seem to mimic?

Ants stretch their bodies when they wake up. They also appear to yawn in a very human manner before taking up the tasks of the day.

How far can a housefly carry germs?

A housefly can transport germs as far as 24.14 kilometres (15 miles) away from the original source of contamination.

For how long can a cockroach live without its head?

A cockroach can live up to nine days without its head.

Do insects have teeth?

Insect teeth are referred to as fangs or mandibles. A mosquito has 47 fangs.

What is the favourite food of cockroaches?

The glue on envelopes and on the back of postage stamps.

Globe Insect

Praying Mantis

What is the proportion of insects on Earth?

Insects make up about 85 per cent of all the animal species on Earth. For every human, there are an estimated 200 million insects!

How many lice can you carry on your body?

More than 3,800 lice can live on one person. In unhygienic situations they can transmit diseases.

Lice

How do butterflies taste their food?

Butterflies have taste sensors located in their feet. They can taste by standing on their food!

What is unusual about the praying mantis?

The praying mantis is the only insect that can turn its head 360 degrees and allows its back to be stroked by humans.

How do mosquitoes make the whining buzz?

That annoying, whining buzz mosquitoes make is the result of a wing beat rate of nearly 600 times per second.

How many flowers does a honeybee visit for a tablespoon of honey?

A honeybee must visit 4,000 flowers to make one tablespoon of honey. In other words, it taps two million flowers for 0.45 kilograms (1 lb) of honey.

the age of the dinosaurs

What was the Mesozoic Era?

Dinosaurs lived throughout most of the Mesozoic Era, which is divided into three periods — Triassic, Jurassic and Cretaceous. The Triassic Period lasted from about 248 million to 213 million years ago. The Jurassic lasted from about 213 million to 145 million years ago, and the Cretaceous from about 145 million to 65 million years ago.

When did dinosaurs live on earth?

Dinosaurs lived from the Triassic period (about 230 million years ago) until the end of the Mesozoic Era (about 65 million years ago).

Dinosaurs were one of several kinds of prehistoric reptiles

What kind of habitat did dinosaurs live in?

They lived on land in nearly all kinds of natural settings — from open plains to forests to the edges of swamps, lakes and oceans.

How long did dinosaurs live on the Earth?

The dinosaurs ruled the Earth for about 165 million years.

What is the meaning of 'dinosaur'?

'Dinosaur' comes from Greek and means 'terrible lizard'.

What kind of animals did dinosaurs evolve from?

The dinosaurs evolved from the codonts, which were a type of archosaur.

How long did dinosaurs take to evolve from reptiles?

The first reptiles appeared during the Carboniferous period, around 340 million years ago. The first dinosaurs appeared around 100 million years later.

Could dinosaurs fly?

The dinosaurs could not fly, though some bird-like dinosaurs seemed to have what looked like feathers.

How did dinosaurs differ from reptiles?

The unique hip structure of the dinosaurs caused their legs to stick out under their bodies and not sprawl on their sides like reptiles.

Did dinosaurs walk on two legs or four legs?

When the dinosaurs evolved they walked on two legs. Much later, some dinosaur groups returned to a four-legged stance, most having rear legs larger than front legs.

What were archosaurs?

Archosaur means 'ruling lizard'. It was so named because this group of reptiles was more advanced than others of its time. Archosaurs had developed strong hind legs and long, strong tails, which helped them swim.

What was the texture of dinosaur skin?

Fossilised skin impressions have only been found for a small fraction of the known dinosaurs. Most skin fossils show bumpy skin. Only the huge plant-eaters seem to have had scaly skin.

What did dinosaur eggs look like?

Dinosaur eggs were round or elongated and had hard, brittle shells.

Dinosaur egg

What is the asteroid impact theory?

According to this theory, an asteroid 6-15 kilometres (3.7 - 9.3 miles) in diameter hit the Earth about 65 million years ago.

How could the asteroid impact affect dinosaurs?

The asteroid impact would have penetrated the earth's crust, scattering dust and debris into the atmosphere, causing huge fires, storms with high winds and highly acidic rain, seismic and, perhaps, even volcanic activity. This in turn could have caused chemical changes, increasing concentrations of sulphuric acid, nitric acid, etc. The heat from the impact could have incinerated all life forms in its path.

When did dinosaurs die out?

They disappeared some 65 million years ago.

What is extinction?

Extinction is the process in which groups of organisms (species) die out. Extinction results if the birth rate is less than the death rate.
It is a natural result of evolution.

How could climatic changes lead to the extinction of dinosaurs?

During the Cretaceous period, due to climatic changes, some of the vegetation that dinosaurs ate died. The flowering plants appeared, displacing most conifers and other plants. This affected the dinosaurs as some herbivorous dinosaurs like the Edmontosaurus only ate conifers.

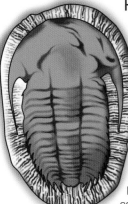

How do we know so much about dinosaurs when they became extinct millions of years ago?

From dinosaurs' fossils.

Most of the knowledge about dinosaurs comes from fossils

Why did dinosaurs become extinct?

Two major theories are given by scientists to explain their extinction — gradual climate changes and the collision of an asteroid with the earth. Most scientists, however, feel that not all dinosaurs became extinct at the end of the Cretaceous period. Many regard birds as living dinosaurs that survived extinction.

Did other creatures become extinct at the same time as the dinosaurs?

Reptiles, like the Pterosaurs in the skies, the Mosasaurs and Plesiosaurs in the water became extinct at the same time as the dinosaurs.

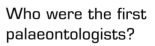

Who were the first palaeontologists?

Dinosaurs were recognised as extinct reptiles only about 200 years ago. It was in 1841 that a man called Sir Richard Owen first gave them the name dinosaurs.

What can the teeth fossils tell about a dinosaur?

Dinosaur teeth fossils can tell the type of food it ate, how it obtained the food and how much further digestion was required i.e. whether it chewed it, or just swallowed it.

What are fossils?

A dead animal turns into a fossil after it remains buried under rocks for millions of years.

What are trace fossils?

Trace fossils record the movements and behaviour of the dinosaurs. These may be tracks (set of footprints), tooth marks, coprolites (fossilised faeces) etc.

What categories are the fossils divided into?

These are divided into two categories: fossilised body parts and fossilised traces.

Which was the first dinosaur fossil found?

The first dinosaur fossil found in the US was a thighbone found by Dr. Caspar Wistar, in Gloucester County, New Jersey, in 1787 (it has since been lost, but more fossils were later found in the area).

What is palaeontology?

Palaeontology is the branch of archaeology that studies fossil organisms and related remains.

What are fossilised body parts?

The most common body fossils found are from the hard parts of the body, including bones, claws and teeth. More rarely, fossils have been found of softer body tissues.

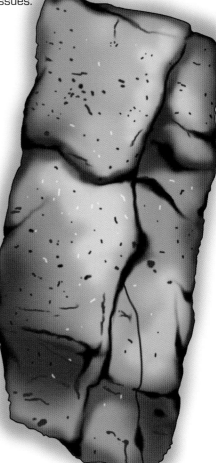

Sedimentary rocks

How are fossils formed?

When an animal dies and is buried in mud over a very long time, the mud hardens and more mud is layered on top. Eventually, it hardens into rock. Then, over millions of years, the rock gradually wears away due to changes in weather, revealing fossilised bones.

What kinds of rock preserve fossils?

Most fossils are preserved in sedimentary rocks like sandstone, shale or limestone.

How many species of dinosaur are known?

There are about 700 described dinosaur species. Every few months a new species is unearthed.

Hadrosaurus

Which dinosaurs are categorised as Ornithischians?

The word 'Ornithischian' means 'bird-hipped'. These dinosaurs had a bird-like hip structure. All Ornithischians were plant-eating dinosaurs and were smaller than Saurischians.

Which dinosaurs were classified as Saurischians?

The word 'Saurischian' means 'lizard-hipped' and this group had a hip formation much like lizards. They included both meat-eating dinosaurs and huge four-legged plant-eating dinosaurs.

Which dinosaurs are examples of the Saurischians?

The Tyrannosaurus Rex, Diplodocus and Brachiosaurus are some of the examples of Saurischians.

Diplodocus

What are the groups that the dinosaurs are divided into?

Scientists divide dinosaurs into two major groups — Ornithischians and Saurischians.

Which dinosaurs are examples of the Ornithischians?

Hadrosauras, Triceratops, and Stegosaurids are some examples of Ornithischians.

Which category do the oldest known dinosaurs fall under?

The oldest known dinosaurs — Eoraptor and Herrerasaurus — are Saurischians, and date from the mid-to-late Triassic period, about 230 million years ago.

What classes were Saurischians further divided into?

The Saurischians were further divided into the Sauropodomorpha —four-legged herbivores — and the Theropods — two-legged carnivores.

Eoraptor

Were the Ornithischians the ancestors of the birds?

In spite of the fact that Ornithischians are said to have a birdlike hip structure, the Saurischians were the actual ancestors of the birds.

Which dinosaur had the highest EQ?

The Troodontids (like Troodon) were probably the smartest dinosaurs; followed by the Dromaeosaurid dinosaurs that had the highest EQ among the dinosaurs.

How is EQ measured?

EQ is the ratio of the brain weight of the animal to the brain weight of a typical animal of the same body weight.

Trodon

What could have been some of the uses of a dinosaur tail?

Scientists have suggested that dinosaurs may have used their tails for purposes such as counterbalance, as a tripod leg or for bludgeoning their enemies.

Which dinosaur had teeth shaped like a human hand?

Ankylosaurs had teeth that were shaped like a human hand with the fingers together.

Dinosaur Teeth

What is EQ?

The EQ or the Encephalization Quotient is a simple way of measuring an animal's intelligence.

Did some dinosaurs have a second brain?

Earlier palaeontologists had mistaken an enlargement of the spinal cord in the hip area of some Sauropods to be a second brain. It is now believed that this enlargement, perhaps containing fat and nerve tissue, may have controlled the animal's hind legs and tail and was larger than the animal's tiny brain.

Synosauropteryx

How did the dinosaur tail help in counter-balance?

The large mass at the front of the dinosaur's body (neck and head) could be counter balanced by its huge, weighty tail so that it did not tip over.

Were the dinosaur tails prehensile?

A prehensile tail is adapted for grasping by wrapping around an object. Some people theorise that dinosaur tails may have been prehensile and used to build nests, or move vegetation and so on, like an elephant's trunk.

What happened if a dinosaur lost or broke its teeth?

They had replaceable teeth, so when a tooth was lost another one grew in its place.

Which dinosaurs did not have any teeth?

Ornithomimids had no teeth, only beaks, with which they ate plants, insects and other small animals

Which dinosaur had weapons on its thumb?

The Iguanodon had spiked thumb weapons and a beak. It used the thumb weapons to stab its predator in the neck, thus making it bleed profusely. The Muttaburrasaurus and the Ouranosaurus were other dinosaurs which had magnificent thumb spikes on each hand.

What did the Troodon use for a weapon?

Troodons had a large retractable claw on one toe of each foot to serve as an ideal weapon for stabbing at a victim.

Which dinosaur had a spiked tail?

The four pointed spikes on the tail of the Stegosaurus could rip into the flesh of its attacker.

What weapons did the Triceratops have?

The Triceratops used its three horns to fight an enemy, the two main ones measuring all of 90 centimetres (3ft.) in length. They would charge at a predator, digging these weapons deep into its flesh.

Which dinosaur had a tail club to fend off his enemies?

The Ankylosaurus had the most magnificent tail-club, one of the strongest dinosaur weapons of all. One swipe would have been enough to sweep the enemy off his feet.

Which dinosaur wore a frill?

The Protoceratops had a frill extending from its neck, like a round collar, which would have protected its body like a shield. It also had a large thick tail to whack its enemies.

Stegosaurus

Which dinosaur had head armour?

The Pachycephalosaurus had a large, thick domed skull which was a form of head armour. It could head-butt anything that might attack it.

Which dinosaur had an armoured body to protect itself and a tail club to attack?

The Euoplocephalus had a well-armoured body to protect itself from its enemies' attacks. Enemies would need to turn it over to wound it. It used its large tail club to attack its predators.

Oviraptor

How did an Oviraptor defend himself from predators?

Oviraptors had 8 centimetres (3 in) long claws on their fingers. They also had claws on their feet and had a toothless beak that may have helped them defend themselves.

Which was the weapon used by Styracosaurus to fight its enemies?

Styracosaurus had a very prominent nose horn to ward off its rivals. The head was surrounded by a huge frill from which six large spines rose.

Pachycephalosaurus

How are dinosaurs named?

Dinosaurs are, generally, named after a characteristic body feature, after the place where they were found, or after a person involved in the discovery. Usually, the name consists of two Greek or Latin words.

Why was the Brachiosaurus so called?

The Brachiosaurus was so named because it had front legs that were longer than its hind legs, which pointed its long neck upward. It had a shorter tail than most other big long-necked dinosaurs. The literal meaning of its name is 'High-chested arm lizard'.

What does the name Tyrannosaurus Rex mean?

Tyrannosaurus means 'Tyrant lizard king'. It is believed to be one of the fiercest meat-eating dinosaurs that ever lived.

Which dinosaur was named after its pretty jaw?

The Compsognathus is a small dinosaur that ate bugs and small lizards. It had an elegant jaw after which it was named.

Which dinosaur was named because of its thick head?

Pachycephalosaurus means 'thick-headed lizard'. It had a domed skull, which was very thick on top and surrounded by lots of bony pieces for protection.

Did the Pentaceratops actually have five horns?

Though the name means 'Five horned face', Pentaceratops was not named so because it had five horns, but because it had longer spike-like cheek projections than other Ceratopsians. This dinosaur had a very large frill, which may have been used as a display against frontal threats.

Pentaceratops

What does 'Maiasaura' mean?

Maiasaura means ' Good mother lizard'. It was given this name because there is evidence that it looked after its young very well.

Why was a Gryposaurus so called?

Gryposaurus means 'Hook-nosed lizard'. It was a large plant-eater that would have travelled in herds while trying to avoid being eaten by some of the earliest Tyrannosaur family members.

What does Oviraptor mean?

The name means 'egg robber'. When it was first discovered, the Oviraptor was sitting on a nest of eggs. Discoverers thought it was stealing the eggs of another dinosaur. Years later, it was found that the eggs were its own.

Spinosaurus

Why was Spinosaurus so named?

The name Spinosaurus means 'Spined Lizard'. It had a huge sail-like structure on its back, which perhaps helped it to survive the climate in that part of the world in the Cretaceous times.

What did the name Triceratops tell about it?

Triceratops means 'Three horned face'. It had a huge frilled head with horns over each eye that could reach over 4 feet long and a third, smaller horn on its nose.

Which was the largest dinosaur?

The biggest dinosaurs were Sauropods. They were gigantic, slow-moving, tiny-headed, cow-like plant-eaters from the late Jurassic period and the early Cretaceous period. They had very long necks, which were counter-balanced by a massive tail.

Which was the first dinosaur to be described scientifically?

The first dinosaur to be scientifically described was the Megalosaurus. The first dinosaur found was the Iguanodon, but it was named and described later than the Megalodon.

Which was the biggest meat-eating dinosaur?

The biggest meat-eating dinosaurs were Theropods from the Cretaceous period. A Theropod called Giganotosaurus Carolinii was found in Patagonia, Argentina, and was 47 ft long (14 m), 8 tons in weight, and 12 ft tall (4 m).

Which was the tallest dinosaur?

The tallest dinosaurs were Brachiosaurid Sauropods. They had front legs that were longer than their back legs and had a giraffe-like stance. They were slow moving herbivores.

Why was the Irritator given its name?

The people who found the fossil of the Irritator added plaster to it in order to make it look more impressive. This nonsense didn't fool the palaeontologists, but irritated them, hence the name.

Megalosaurus

Which was the biggest carnivore?

The Gigantosaurus — it was 14 metres (45.93 ft) long, 4 metres (13.12 ft) tall and weighed 8 tons.

Which was the broadest dinosaur?

The broadest were Ankylosaurids. From the late Cretaceous, these plated dinosaurs were slow-moving herbivores with a club-like tail. They were tremendously heavy.

Which was the smallest dinosaur egg ever found?

The smallest dinosaur eggs are just a few inches across and tennis ball-shaped, but we don't know which dinosaur laid them.

Which dinosaur had the longest neck?

The Mamenchisaurus, a plant-eater, had what is thought to be the world's longest neck ever, extending all of 10m (32ft). Its neck extended to more than half its total body length and measured more than eight times the height of today's average adult man.

Which is the longest dinosaur name of all?

Micropachycephalosaurus is the longest of the dinosaur names. It means 'tiny thick-headed lizard'.

Mamenchisaurus

Which was the fastest dinosaur?

It is difficult to kno w the exact speeds but the fastest dinosaurs probably ran over 70 kilometres per hour (40 mph). These included the Gallimimus, the Ornithomimus, the Coelophysis and the Velociraptor.

Velociraptor

Which was the heaviest dinosaur?

The Ultrasaurus, a late Jurassic dinosaur, may have weighed as much as 55 tons — many times heavier than elephants today.

Which was the oldest dinosaur ever found?

The Staurikosaurus lived over 230 million years ago in South Africa. It may have been related to the giant meat-eating dinosaurs of the Jurassic and Cretaceous periods.

Which was the longest dinosaur?

The Diplodocus, a 'lizard-hipped' dinosaur, which was a Sauropod, was the longest of the land animals but not the heaviest. The largest Diplodocus is noted as weighing 15 tons and being 27 metres (88.58 ft) long.

Which was the richest dinosaur area?

Dinosaur Provincial Park in Alberta, Canada, has yielded 35 separate dinosaur species to date.

Which dinosaur wore a helmet?

Corythosaurus, meaning 'helmeted lizard' gets its name from the bony crest on top of its head similar to the helmets worn by ancient Corinthian warriors.

Which was the smallest dinosaur?

The smallest dinosaur yet discovered is the Compsognathus, which was the size of a chicken! It was a bird-like dinosaur that walked on two long, thin legs with three-toed feet. They were 0.7-1.4 metres (28 in-4.6 ft) long meat eaters that caught and ate small animals, including insects and lizards.

Whose are the largest eggs ever found?

Those of the Hyselosaurus, which lived some 80 million years ago. The eggs, measuring 300 x 255 millimetres (11 x 10 in), were discovered in Southern France in 1961.

Which dinosaur had the most teeth?

The Hadrosaurs (duck-billed dinosaurs) had nearly 1000 cheek teeth!

Which dinosaur had the longest life span?

The huge Sauropods, long-necked plant-eaters with small heads and long tails from the Jurassic period, are estimated to have had a life-span of about 100 years.

Composognathus

Which was the mightiest dinosaur?

With an amazing armoured head and body, the Ankylosaurus was built like a tank. Reinforcement was provided by several rows of nasty looking plates and spikes. Its powerful tail, too, ended in a curious, two-sectioned bone.

Ankylosaurus

Were all huge, prehistoric animals dinosaurs?

Not all prehistoric animals were dinosaurs. A lot of other animals existed during the Mesozoic period along with the dinosaurs. Some animals were closely related to the dinosaurs, like the Pterosaurs. Other animals, like the Dimetrodon, which lived in the Paleozoic Era before the dinosaurs existed, are more closely related to us than to the dinosaurs.

Pterosaurus

Had dinosaurs really become extinct 65 million years ago?

Most of the dinosaur groups became extinct long before the mass extinction of 65 million years ago. The remaining dinosaurs died out at that time, but many bird species survived it.

Did dinosaurs lose out in the survival game?

No. In fact dinosaurs ruled the Earth for about 165 million years. In comparison, humans have only been around for about a million years. In terms of survival through geological time, dinosaurs were long-lasting animals, probably leaving birds as their descendants.

Were dinosaurs slow and sluggish animals?

Early palaeontologists thought dinosaurs must have been slow and sluggish to have lost the evolutionary race to birds and mammals. Modern studies find no sign that they were laggards, lazily dragging their tails behind them. Most dinosaurs were probably as mobile as large, modern mammals.

Did any dinosaurs swim or fly?

There were no flying or swimming dinosaurs. All dinosaurs lived on land; none of them lived in the seas or flew (until the birds). Neither the flying Pterosaurs, nor the swimming Ichthyosaurs were dinosaurs, although all were closely related.

Did all dinosaurs live and die at the same time?

The dinosaurs roamed the Earth for about 165 million years. Different types of dinosaurs existed at different times. Dinosaur species evolved and became extinct throughout the Mesozoic Era.

Ichthyosaurs

Did humans co-exist with dinosaurs?

Although the image of human cave dwellers hunting dinosaurs is well established in fiction, it is far from accurate. Humans didn't evolve until about 65 million years after the dinosaurs' extinction.

Did mammals exist in the age of dinosaurs?

Tiny mammals lived in the shadow of dinosaurs for more than 150 million years. Synapsids were the ancestors of mammals, which evolved before dinosaurs but lost the evolutionary competition to them. By 295 millions years ago, the remaining Synapsids had shrunk to become mammals as small as two grams, surviving by eating insects and worms rather like today's rodents. Mammals remained small until 65 million years ago, when the death of the dinosaurs left them room to grow.